●= TEAM DECISION-MAKING TECHNIQUES

A Practical Guide To Successful Team Outcomes

P. Keith Kelly

Jossey-Bass
Pfeiffer
San Francisco

RICHARD
CHANG
ASSOCIATES

Published by

JOSSEY-BASS/PFEIFFER

A Wiley Company
350 Sansome St.
San Francisco, CA 94104-1342
415.433.1740; Fax 415.433.0499
800.274.4434; Fax 800.569.0443

| www.pfeiffer.com |

Jossey-Bass/Pfeiffer is a registered trademark of John Wiley & Sons, Inc.

ISBN: 0-7879-5089-0
Library of Congress Catalog Card Number 99-61858

Printed in the United States of America

Printing 10 9 8 7 6 5 4 3 2

We at Jossey-Bass strive to use the most environmentally sensitive paper stocks available to us. Our publications are printed on acid-free recycled stock whenever possible, and our paper always meets or exceeds minimum GPO and EPA requirements.

ACKNOWLEDGMENTS

About The Author

P. Keith Kelly, a Senior Consultant at Richard Chang Associates, Inc., is an experienced educator, consultant, and management professional. His special areas of expertise encompass strategic planning and analysis, financial management, process improvement, and market research.

The author would like to acknowledge the support of the entire team of professionals at Richard Chang Associates, Inc. for their contribution to the guidebook development process. In addition, special thanks are extended to the many client organizations who have helped us shape the practical ideas and proven methods shared in this guidebook.

Additional Credits

Reviewers:	Carole Markin, Jim Greeley, and Dottie Snyder
Graphic Layout:	Suzanne Jamieson
Cover Design:	John Odam Design Associates

PREFACE

The 1990's have already presented individuals and organizations with some very difficult challenges to face and overcome. So who will have the advantage as we move into the 21st century?

The advantage will belong to those with a commitment to continuous learning. Whether on an individual basis or as an entire organization, one key ingredient to building a continuous learning environment is *The Practical Guidebook Collection* brought to you by the Publications Division of Richard Chang Associates, Inc.

After understanding the future "learning needs" expressed by our clients and other potential customers, we are pleased to publish *The Practical Guidebook Collection*. The guidebooks are designed to provide you with proven, "real-world" tips, tools, and techniques— on a wide range of subjects—that you can apply in the workplace and/or on a personal level immediately.

Once you've had a chance to benefit from this book, please refer to the back pages for additional guidebooks available from our *Practical Guidebook Collection* along with additional quality training resources from Richard Chang Associates, Inc.

Wishing you successful reading,

TABLE OF CONTENTS

Nonteam decision:

Decision by far-removed generals and their order to
the Light Brigade: *"Charge!"*
Result—600 dead.

Team decision:

U.S. Men's Olympic ice hockey team at Lake Placid:
"Let's all do our very best!"
Result: Gold medal and the *"Miracle On Ice."*

CHAPTER ONE

INTRODUCTION

If problems didn't exist, there would be no need for decisions. Of course, problems do crop up, and we need to make decisions to solve them. We all find ourselves in situations where choices need to be made and plans need to be formulated. When these decisions are made on an individual basis, the process is fairly simple. But when decisions have to be made with other people, it's a completely different story.

Why Read This Guidebook?

If you've ever worked as part of a group or team, whether in a work team at your office or on a PTA committee, you know how difficult the decision-making process can be. Wouldn't it be nice to have some tools to make the process easier and the results better? *Team Decision-Making Techniques* is a guidebook designed to do just that.

Team Decision-Making Techniques helps you and your team make decisions while minimizing conflict. This guidebook introduces six ways to make team decisions.

Six Ways To Make Team Decisions

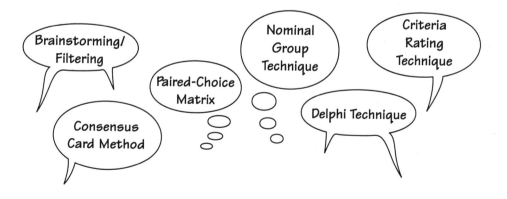

Using one or more of these techniques, you and your team members will be able to make better and faster decisions. Making good decisions in less time will increase your group's effectiveness.

Better
Decisions

Better
Team

Who Should Read This Guidebook?

Team Decision-Making Techniques can help team leaders, team members involved in group decisions, and individuals who facilitate team meetings. It can help you become a more vital participant in your group's decision making.

If you are thinking of joining a team, or are about to join one, this guidebook can give you a sense of how teams interact.

Finally, this guidebook is valuable for people who volunteer time to nonprofit organizations, such as community associations, school boards, professional associations, and so on. The techniques that follow make group meetings and the decision-making process run smoothly.

When And How To Use It

Whether your team is solving a problem or making a decision, the techniques in this guidebook will help you reach a successful outcome. Although problem solving and decision making have different elements *(such as sense of urgency)*, the processes have many similarities as you will note in the upcoming chapters.

Your team can refer to this guidebook when you have a problem to solve and you want to find the most effective and efficient way to solve it. Consult it before and during team meetings on decisions regarding such things as operations and long-term planning.

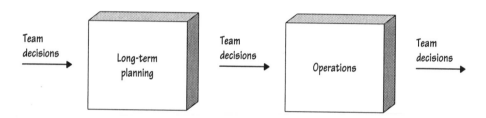

This guidebook can also serve as a refresher to hone team decision-making skills. If you get stuck during the decision-making process *(and discover that the problem is more complex than you expected)*, you can use this guidebook to refocus your group and clarify the decision that needs to be made. You might also use it when an unusual problem arises and your team needs to find a different way to handle it.

Each chapter focuses on a different team decision-making technique. There are step-by-step instructions and practical examples for each method.

Try the exercises in this guidebook, make notes in the margins, share it with coworkers—but don't let it sit on the shelf.

Note: The terms *problem* and *decision* are used interchangeably and equivalently throughout this guidebook.

ABOUT TEAM DECISIONS

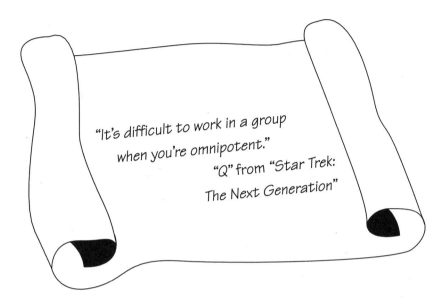

"It's difficult to work in a group when you're omnipotent."

"Q" from "Star Trek: The Next Generation"

What Is Team Decision Making?

In the past, the effective manager was all too often seen as an all-knowing, tough, single-minded individual who made decisions that his or her underlings followed. The successful manager of today and the future is a member of a team that pools its expertise and knowledge to find solutions to a wide range of problems.

Since the structure of the work unit itself is evolving, the team decision-making process is also changing. Although they take more time, group decisions tend to incorporate the maximum amount of data and experience *(both good and bad)*, plus a diversity of opinions. Studies have shown that people who participate in group decisions are more likely to implement them.

To make team decisions, both managers and employees must learn some new ideas and develop new techniques. The first idea all team members must understand is the term *"consensus."* In teams, consensus means, *"We all can live with 'X' as a solution to a problem and we all agree to go along with whatever 'X' requires us to do."*

Tips For Obtaining Consensus

When attempting to reach consensus in your group, try to:

➡ **Be frank and honest when expressing your ideas and opinions.**

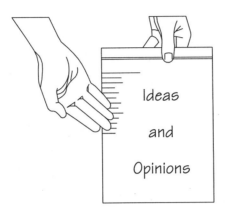

Don't fall into the trap of adjusting your ideas to move with the drift of the discussion.

➡ **Avoid judging ideas instantaneously.**

Let team members state their cases and ask questions. If you punish people for suggesting concepts that are unusual or untested, chances are they will stop participating. The group, as a whole, will lose out. After all, some of the best discoveries in the world were made when least expected.

➠ **Be willing to compromise and be flexible.**

Avoid personality conflicts, power plays, and backroom politicking. Such behavior destroys trust.

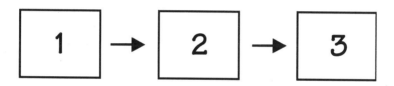

➠ **Examine decisions and problems in a systematic manner.**

Be sure that all team members understand the process you are using.

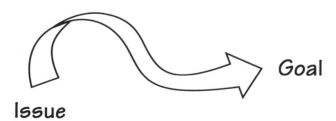

➠ **Agree at the outset on the issue you are tackling and your goal.**

➡ **Make sure all team members have the same information.**

Nothing ruffles feathers more than finding out that other team members received more or different information.

➡ **Allow enough time to reach consensus, but don't allow too much time.**

People may get tired and lose interest in the issue at hand and its outcome(s).

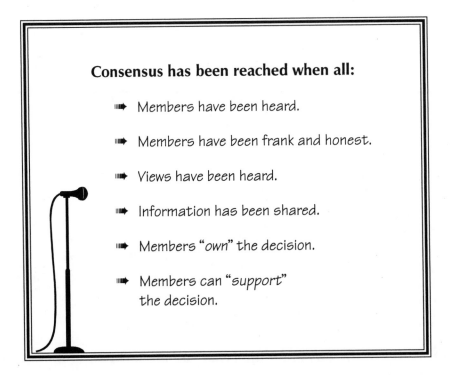

Consensus has been reached when all:

➡ Members have been heard.

➡ Members have been frank and honest.

➡ Views have been heard.

➡ Information has been shared.

➡ Members "own" the decision.

➡ Members can "support" the decision.

Why Are Decisions Made On A Team Basis?

Two heads are better than one. And more than two is even better. If the decision-making process is effective, it pulls together the skills, knowledge, experience, and opinions of your group and produces a solution that is greater than the sum of its parts.

A good decision has two basic components: quality and commitment. A quality decision takes into account all of the facts and makes good use of that information. It's a logical choice with sound reasoning behind it.

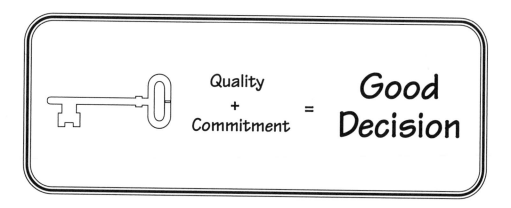

The second element to a good decision is the commitment of the people who have to carry it out. A good decision may be effective and innovative, but if people don't have the commitment to carry it out—for whatever reason—then it is a useless decision.

On the other hand, a poor decision that everyone gladly implements is just as wasteful and counterproductive. For instance, a group may decide that it wants to sponsor a marathon race to foster team spirit. But if no one shows up or trains for the race, then the race will be a disaster, a poor decision.

On the following pages are just a few of the benefits of making decisions on a team basis.

Benefits of team decision making

➠ **Fresh and unusual ideas**

Each person who contributes to a decision-making process has ideas. Some ideas may be fresh, unusual, and different from what you may have come up with on your own. They may spark other, even better, thoughts.

Team
Member # 1

Team
Member # 3

Team
Member # 2

➠ **A chance to minimize misunderstandings and biases**

Each member of a team brings certain biases and preferences to the table. Such biases can be shared, incorporated into the outcome, and any potential misunderstandings cleared up before the solution needs to be implemented.

| Growth | Challenge | Understanding | Results |

➠ **Increased learning and personal growth**

When you make decisions, you have to think. You also have to learn about the underlying issues and make up your own mind about outcomes—you grow!

➠ **Increased challenge and autonomy**

Employees who confront problems and create solutions tend to be more motivated to improve their work and the work of their team. They feel responsible for that work and take steps toward becoming more autonomous.

➠ **Increased understanding of the big picture**

When you are involved in making decisions, you develop a better understanding of other decisions made throughout your organization. You understand the difficulties and trade-offs of choosing between conflicting options.

➠ **Better results**

Since most decisions require many people for implementation, a team decision is more likely to promote better results.

What Kinds Of Decisions Should Be Made On A Team Basis?

All decisions do not need to be made on a team basis. Some decisions are best made by an individual, or with some input from others. One way to judge a successful manager in today's environment is his or her ability to determine which decisions should be made by the group and which should be made individually.

In general, decisions should be made on a team basis if:

➡ The outcome affects everyone in the group.

➡ The solution is critical for the team's customers since customer satisfaction is based on the efforts of a team, not an individual effort.

➡ The solution has long-term implications.

➡ It is a sensitive issue, and team members need to know and understand how such a decision was reached. Sensitive issues might include affirmative action, scheduling, and discipline.

CHAPTER TWO WORKSHEET: MAKING TEAM DECISIONS

1. What decision-making techniques are currently being used by your team?

_____

_____

_____

2. Are they effective?

_____

_____

3. Why or why not?

_____

_____

_____

4. What benefits would there be for your team to use structured team decision-making techniques?

_____

_____

_____

BRAINSTORMING/FILTERING

What Is Brainstorming/Filtering?

Brainstorming/Filtering can be used to tap your group's creativity. It helps you generate many ideas, or possible alternatives, from which to make a group decision.

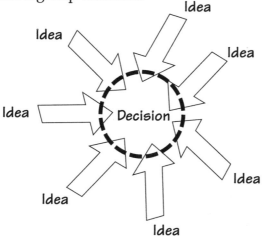

Teams use brainstorming as a consensus-building tool and when they need to generate a large number of ideas. Filtering reduces the list of brainstormed ideas to a manageable number or to the point of deciding on a course of action.

When Should Brainstorming/Filtering Be Used?

Teams and departments should use brainstorming when:

- ☞ **Determining possible causes and/or solutions to problems.**

- ☞ **Planning the steps of a team project.**

- ☞ **Deciding problems or improvement opportunities to work on.**

- ☞ **Nonroutine decisions must be made that require special creativity.**

- ☞ **The team wants to include all options.**

The Six Steps Of Brainstorming/Filtering

Step 1: Prepare for the Brainstorming/Filtering session

Step 2: Determine the brainstorming method to use

Step 3: Generate ideas

Step 4: Create filters

Step 5: Apply filters

Step 6: Wrap up the Brainstorming/ Filtering session

Let's look at an example . . .

of how Brainstorming/Filtering worked for a problem-solving team at Sports Outfitters Inc.

When Sports Outfitters, Inc. purchased Backwoods Wear, the boss wanted Tina, the leader of a problem-solving group, to come up with ways to bring the Backwoods Wear employees into the Sports Outfitters' fold. Because the merger was unexpected, Tina and her team needed to devise a plan right away. Tina felt the best way to accomplish this was to schedule a Brainstorming/Filtering session. She chose this method because, in her experience, it had been effective in generating a wide range of possibilities and bringing about consensus on the best course of action. . . .

Step 1: Prepare for the Brainstorming/Filtering session

➡ Provide a time limit for the session (*generally 30 minutes is sufficient*).

➡ Identify a Facilitator/Recorder. The Recorder's job is to write all ideas down where everyone can see them (*on a flip chart or overhead transparency*). The Recorder also encourages participation and makes sure that the ground rules governing the session are followed.

➡ Establish the ground rules.

Tina and her group . . .

decided to spend 20 minutes brainstorming and 20 minutes filtering. Don volunteered to be the Recorder. Tina reminded the group of the ground rules for brainstorming, such as:

➡ Don't criticize ideas, even the most outrageous ideas anyone might voice.

➡ Don't edit what is said.

➡ Go for quantity of ideas at this point; narrow down the list later using the filtering technique.

➡ Encourage wild, exaggerated and humorous ideas. Creativity is the key here.

➡ Build on the ideas of others (*e.g., one member might say something that "sparks" another member's idea*).

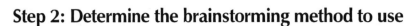

Step 2: Determine the brainstorming method to use

Choose either the *"freewheeling"* or *"round-robin"* method of brainstorming.

Brainstorming Methods	
Freewheeling	**Round-Robin**
Share ideas simultaneously.	Everyone takes a turn offering an idea.
List all ideas as they are "shouted out."	Anyone can pass on any turn.
	Continue until there are no more ideas.
	All ideas are listed as they are offered.

Since the group was in a chatty mood . . .
Tina decided to go with a freewheeling approach to brainstorming. She explained to the group, *"Anyone can shout out an idea anytime it comes to you."* . . .

Step 3: Generate ideas

Generate as many ideas as possible. Certain clues will help you determine when to stop your Brainstorming/Filtering session.

Stop brainstorming when:

➠ Everyone has had a chance to participate.

➠ No more ideas are offered.

➠ You have made a "last call" for ideas.

➠ You have thanked team members for their input and time.

Tina started the session . . .

by offering an idea that Don recorded on the flip chart. After that, three team members shouted ideas in rapid succession. Then the group fell silent. Tina thought, *"We've only come up with four ideas and we need at least 20. Perhaps I should change the way we're brainstorming, from a freewheeling session to the more structured, round-robin method? That might help create more ideas."*

Tina announced that from now on they would go around the table clockwise and ask each person to offer one idea. If someone didn't have an idea, then they could *"pass the ball"* to the person on their right.

The group switched to the round-robin technique, and within three minutes they generated another 20 ideas.

They listed their ideas for bringing Backwoods Wear employees into the Sports Outfitters' fold. . . .

Establish employee buddy system.

Hold monthly lunches for new and old employees.

Celebrate birthdays for all new employees.

Ask new employees to offer systems input.

Invite new employees to join Sports Outfitters' sports teams.

Meet to review the organization's structure and history.

Prepare glossary of special terms used by Sports Outfitters.

Construct work teams made up of 50 percent new and 50 percent existing employees.

Familiarize new employees with all product lines and labels.

Make an orientation video.

Ask new employees to make a list of their expectations and preconceptions.

Tina stopped the team . . .

and thanked them for their energy and ideas. She then announced that it was time to begin the second step of the process, called the filtering session. . . .

Step 4: Create filters

Filters are sets of criteria or constraints that help you evaluate alternatives. You can use filters to edit out or edit in choices. When creating filters, you should use whatever criteria and constraints are appropriate and applicable to the specific decision your team is making.

Here are some common filters:

 Cost—too high; within budget

 Time—can be done by target date; complete this quarter

 Availability—have the resources in-house

 Fit—with our way of doing things/philosophy; with our market and image

 Customer impact—will have a direct positive impact; will be negative

 Resistance to idea versus acceptability— minimal resistance; acceptable to management

 Practicality—in terms of approach

Tina told her team . . .

that it was time to narrow their choices and explained that she wanted them to use the filtering method to decide on ideas they would recommend to management. To do that, the group would need to come up with four filters that could be used to edit out ideas or to edit them in. Susan rattled off three filters: *"No people, doesn't disrupt work, no time."* Bill added the issue of no cost to the company, *or "no money."*

Tina applauded their suggestions. Don listed the four filters on a separate piece of paper that he hung on the wall next to the original list of brainstorming ideas. . . .

Filters

No time—get team up to speed ASAP.

No money—doesn't favor new employees, doesn't incur more debt.

No people—should utilize existing staff only.

Doesn't disrupt work—doesn't alter current systems or operations.

Step 5: Apply filters

Apply filters one at a time to each idea on the list. Cross out any ideas that do not pass through each filter *(or check them off if you are using the "filtering in" approach).* Every filter will select a different set of items.

Continue applying filters until the desired number of choices emerge.

Tina asked Susan . . .

to serve as Recorder for the filtering session. Susan took a blue marker and crossed out all ideas that did not fit with the filter *"no time."* Starting at the top, she reviewed the list and used an orange marker to cross out all ideas that did not fit with the second filter, *"no money."* With a purple marker, she crossed out ideas that did not fit with the third filter, *"no people."* She used a green marker to cross out ideas that did not fit with the fourth filter, *"doesn't disrupt work."* When she was finished, only a handful of ideas remained.

Tina read off the three remaining items and asked how the team felt about the decision to present these recommendations to management. . . .

List of ideas that survived all four filters:

➠ Establish employee buddy system.

➠ Invite new employees to join Sports Outfitters' sports teams.

➠ Construct work teams made up of 50 percent new and 50 percent existing employees.

Step 6: Wrap up the Brainstorming/Filtering session

Review the ideas that survived the filtering process. Define each of them to make sure all team members agree on these ideas. The group should also delegate a representative to pass on the information to the appropriate parties inside and outside your organization.

Buddy system

Work teams

Sports teams

Tina thanked Susan for her help . . .

with the filtering and asked the group to look at the three ideas that remained on the chart. Tina then asked Barbara and Bill to define them. Everyone agreed that Tina should report the findings to management as a decision made and supported by the entire team.

SUMMARY

In summary, use Brainstorming/Filtering to:

☑ **Analyze problems.**

Brainstorming helps the team generate a large quantity of ideas, and filtering helps to narrow down this long list of ideas to arrive at a team decision on a solution.

☑ **Plan team projects.**

Although not the primary use of this tool, brainstorming can be used to help identify different steps in implementing a project.

☑ **Making decisions outside the normal range of team decisions.**

Brainstorming/Filtering requires the active involvement of all team members and can be used to signal to team members that the decision being made requires special treatment.

☑ **Cover all options.**

Brainstorming ensures that as many ideas as possible are brought into the decision-making process.

CHAPTER THREE WORKSHEET:
USING BRAINSTORMING/FILTERING

1. What types of decisions does your team make as a group?

_____

_____

_____

_____

2. List the specific opportunities you have to use Brainstorming/ Filtering as a team decision-making technique.

_____

_____

_____

_____

3. Which brainstorming method will work best for your team decisions, and why?

❑ Freewheeling. Why?

_____

❑ Round-robin. Why?

_____

4. Which *"ground rules"* should be used in the situations you listed above? Why?

☐   No judging, evaluating or criticizing

_____

☐   Go for quantity

_____

☐   Be creative

_____

☐   Build on ideas

_____

☐   Build a visible record of ideas

_____

5. Which is the most effective filtering technique for your team to use, and why?

_____

_____

6. Which filters might your team use most often?

_____

_____

_____

NOMINAL GROUP TECHNIQUE

What Is The Nominal Group Technique?

The Nominal Group Technique *(NGT)* combines aspects of silent voting with limited discussion to help you build consensus and arrive at a team decision.

When Should The NGT Be Used?

Use the NGT when:

☞ **Dealing with a sensitive, controversial, or prominent issue and you think contrary opinions and a myriad of details may paralyze the discussion.** *(Using the NGT, the first round of ideas is generated silently, so discussion is held off until all ideas have been presented.)*

☞ **You want to ensure equal participation by all team members.** *(Using the NGT, each member has an equal opportunity to contribute, regardless of rank, seniority, or personality.)*

☞ **A team has identified the root cause of a problem, but identifying a course of action from many alternatives is difficult.**

The Seven Steps Of The NGT

Step 1: Define the problem to be solved or the decision to be made

Step 2: Silently generate ideas

Step 3: State and record ideas

Step 4: Clarify each item on the list

Step 5: Rank items silently; list rankings

Step 6: Tally rankings

Step 7: Wrap up the NGT session

Now let's look at an example of how the NGT works for a team deciding how to improve team performance.

Improving
Team
Performance

Step 1: Define the problem to be solved or decision to be made

The problem, or decision, should be clearly defined and understood at the beginning of the session. Post a brief but complete statement outlining the problem/decision so all team members can read it.

Bob's team knew . . .

it was not doing as well as the other sales groups within their pharmaceutical company. To determine what the team should do, Bob decided to hold an idea-generating session using the NGT.

On a flip chart, Bob recorded what he felt was a clear statement of the decision the team had to address. *"What are the critical things we should do to make our team function as a high-performance team?"* Bob's seven team members agreed with this starting point. . . .

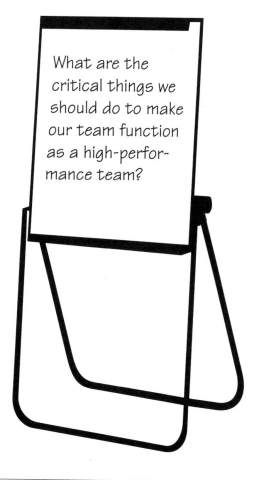

What are the
critical things we
should do to make
our team function
as a high-perfor-
mance team?

Step 2: Silently generate ideas

Silently and independently, each team member writes down his or her ideas on how to make improvements. Ideas should be kept to a few words or a short phrase. The team can work within a five-minute time limit, or each member can try to come up with 10 or 12 ideas.

Bob passed out index cards . . .

and asked each team member to write down as many things as they could in the next five minutes that might improve team performance. . . .

Step 3: State and record ideas

In round-robin fashion, team members should offer one idea from their lists. The Recorder simultaneously writes the ideas on a flip chart or board visible to the group. The round-robin process continues until each person has given all of his or her ideas. The Recorder should not duplicate items. If items are combined, the Recorder should make sure the team agrees that the ideas are, in fact, related.

At this point, team members still don't discuss ideas; that comes in the next step.

During this phase, team members are encouraged to *"piggyback."* A person hitchhikes by thinking of a new idea after hearing another member's idea. Everyone is encouraged to add new ideas to the list and offer them on their next turn.

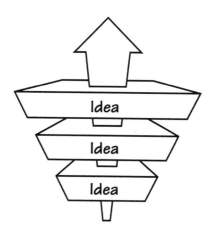

Standing at the flip chart . . .

Bob went around the room asking each of his team members to offer one idea from the bunch they'd written down on index cards. As Diane listened to her teammates offering ideas, she realized that most of her ideas were mentioned by other people before Bob had a chance to call on her. Wanting to participate in the process, Diane thought, *"What can I add to this list?"* She read through the items on the flip chart again. This time a new idea came to her. Diane mused, *"Seeing the other good ideas on the flip chart 'sparked' my imagination."*. . .

Here is the list of ideas they generated using the NGT:

Survey customers on wants and needs.

Practice sessions with other workers.

Prioritize products to sell.

Target key buyers and take them to lunch.

Try team selling—the one-two sales punch.

Give a prize to the person who sells the most.

Review the team's dress code.

Develop a standard team sales pitch that can be tailored.

Figure out what is unique about our team.

Determine which products don't sell and drop them.

Distribute more free samples.

Step 4: Clarify each item on the list

For each item on the list from Step 3, allow an equal amount of time for group discussion. The objective here is to clarify each idea in case the wording is not clear, and not to win arguments. This step should be led by a group leader or facilitator. The leader reads each idea aloud, asks if there are any questions, and is responsible for keeping the group moving through the list.

Clarify Each Item

Bob reviewed the items . . .

aloud and asked if there were any questions about the meaning or wording of each item. At times, he asked volunteers to give their *"definitions"* of the phrases on the flip chart. Team members disagreed on the meaning of several phrases. They clarified them and then moved on. . . .

Step 5: Rank items silently; list rankings

Assign a letter to each idea listed on the flip chart. For example, if you end up with six ideas, then you have statements labeled, "*A, B, C, D, E, F.*"

Ask each team member to write down the letters corresponding to those listed on the flip chart.

Bob's team . . .
labeled the eleven ideas they had come up with "*A through K.*". . .

A: Survey customers on wants and needs.

B: Practice sessions with other workers.

C: Prioritize products to sell.

D: Target key buyers and take them to lunch.

E: Try team selling—the one-two sales punch.

F: Give a prize to the person who sells the most.

G: Review the team's dress code.

H: Develop a standard team sales pitch that can be tailored.

I: Figure out what is unique about our team.

J: Determine which products don't sell and drop them.

K: Distribute more free samples.

Ask each team member to vote silently for the idea that best solves the problem or addresses the issue you are deciding. Assign a *"1"* to that idea. Assign a *"2"* to the second best idea, and so on. The higher the number, the less important the idea is to the individual who is silently voting.

As an alternative, if there is a long list of ideas to rank *(more than a dozen)* the team may use the *"half plus one"* rule. This rule suggests ranking only half of the items generated by the group, plus one. For example, if there were 30 items on the list, they would rank 16 of them in descending order of importance—from 1 to 16.

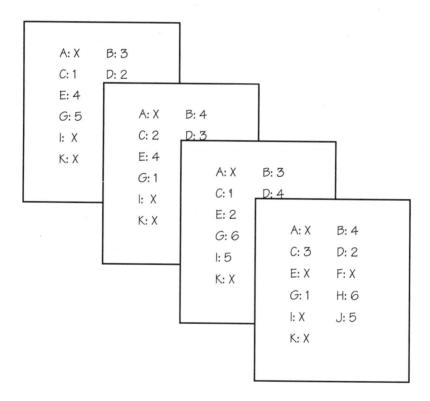

The team agreed with Bob . . .
that they should focus on assigning a rank to only six items out of the 11 they had generated. . . .

Step 6: Tally rankings

In this step, each team member calls out their rankings. The Recorder lists them on a flip chart.

Add up each line of numbers horizontally. The item with the lowest total represents the team's decision up to this point—prior to discussion of the merits of the ideas.

A:	6	5	1	4	4	5	3	4	= 32
B:	4	3	2	2	3	2	3	4	= 23
☞ C:	1	2	3	1	2	1	3	2	= 15
D:	3	1	4	6	4	3	5	2	= 28

Bob and his team . . .

tallied the scores and weren't surprised to see what came out on top: *"prioritize products to sell."* This had been mentioned many times before, as had most of the other items, but this was the first time the team had actually used any kind of formal process to see where they stood as a team on the issue. . . .

Step 7: Wrap up the NGT session

List the items your team has agreed upon in descending order on a flip chart or board. Clarify again the definitions of the items. Discuss the vote openly. The purpose of the discussion is to find out if the final vote seems consistent and to reconsider items that may have received the wrong number (*too few or too many*) of votes. If things seem inconsistent, you might want to vote again.

Choose the next course of action and assign tasks to the appropriate team members. Thank everyone for their time, energy, ideas and cooperation.

Moira, one of the team members, asked . . .

"Does everybody really agree that prioritizing products to sell is the most important thing for us to do?" After a few minutes of discussion the team agreed they could start work right away on the top two items on their list. They could tackle two of the others after the quarterly data came in. They also decided to drop one item and meet with management regarding the remaining point. Everyone agreed that the NGT process produced team decisions with a minimum of conflict, yet allowed discussion of the pros and cons of the alternatives.

Prioritize

products

to sell

SUMMARY

In summary, use the Nominal Group Technique to . . .

☑ Generate alternatives and choose a course of action.

☑ Minimize opinions and *"politicking"* over the decision-making process.

☑ Foster team member commitment to a decision through equal involvement in the decision-making process.

CHAPTER FOUR WORKSHEET:
USING THE NOMINAL GROUP TECHNIQUE

1. a) In which specific situations would your team use the NGT?

_____

_____

_____

_____

b) Why?

_____

_____

_____

_____

2. Define the problem to be solved or the decision that needs to be made for one of these situations.

_____

_____

_____

_____

3. Who needs to be involved in this team decision?

_____

_____

_____

_____

4. Will your team use a time limit or a target number of ideas in Step 2?

_____

_____

_____

❑ Time Limit. Why?

_____

_____

_____

❑ Target number of ideas. Why?

_____

_____

_____

5. Who will record these ideas for the team to see?

_____

_____

6. Who will make sure the ideas are all clearly defined?

_____

_____

7. Who will facilitate the discussion after the ideas have been rated by everyone and the ratings tallied?

_____

_____

8. What action items need to be taken care of to make sure the team's decision is carried out?

_____

_____

_____

_____

_____

_____

THE DELPHI TECHNIQUE

Round 1

Input
Input
Input
Input
Input
Input
Input

Round 2

Input
Input
Input
Input

Round 3

Input

What Is The Delphi Technique?

The Delphi Technique involves the solicitation and comparison of multiple rounds of anonymous judgments from team members on a decision or problem. Each round provides members with a summary of what all team members said in the previous round and solicits a new round of inputs. By the end of three rounds, your group should reach consensus.

A very public example of the Delphi Technique of voting is the Academy Awards. Members of the Academy *(without consultation with other members)* nominate whomever they want in particular categories *(e.g., actor, actress, picture, etc.)* and send that ballot to the Academy. The Academy determines which five got the highest number of votes in each category and distributes that new list to the group. Then the group votes again.

When Should The Delphi Technique Be Used?

Use the Delphi Technique when:

- ☞ **You want the input of several team members while removing the biasing effect of face-to-face contact.**

- ☞ **The team members are not in the same location.**

- ☞ **The decision requires all members to *"buy into"* the outcome and the evolution of that outcome.**

- ☞ **You want to avoid the effects of dominant individuals and peer pressure. *(Using the Delphi Technique, responses are anonymous).***

The Eight Steps Of The Delphi Technique

Step 1: Define the decision or problem

Step 2: Team provides Round 1 input

Step 3: Summarize Round 1; ask for Round 2 input

Step 4: Team provides Round 2 input

* **Step 5:** Summarize Round 2; ask for Round 3 input

Step 6: Team provides Round 3 input

Step 7: Summarize Round 3

Step 8: Wrap up the Delphi session

> ***Note:** If consensus is reached at Round 2, Steps 5 and 6 are unnecessary.

Step 1: Define the decision or problem

Before team members can provide their input, the decision, problem, or desired outcome of the process needs to be defined. Some examples of a defined outcome of the Delphi Technique might include:

➠ The team has to decide how much of the bonus pool to pay out this quarter, how much should go into the next quarter's pool, and how this quarter's portion should be shared among the five members.

➠ The team has to agree on the five strategic goals on which to focus over the next three years.

➠ The team has to find a solution to the staff turnover problem.

In addition to defining the decision or problem, the team needs to agree on the process. For example, they may decide in the first Delphi round that each member will contribute five ideas; in the second round, three; and in the final round, only two.

The board members of the Charity Service League . . .

were once again having a tough time agreeing. Their annual meeting was approaching and they wanted to give an award for the best team member of the year. Unfortunately, no one could agree on what *"the best"* really meant. Finally, George, the president of the group, noted, *"If we knew what our organization really stood for, we'd have no trouble devising an award. Therefore, I suggest we sit down and figure out what the mission of our organization really is."* *"Yes,"* added Betty. *"Let's come up with a mission statement—a few sentences that explain why we exist as a group and what we do."* But George was skeptical. *"This board will never agree on anything and it's tough just to get them all in the same room to discuss it."*

Betty told him not to worry. *"If we use the Delphi Technique to create the mission statement, people could participate in the decision from anywhere and they would avoid all the usual face-to-face battles we've had in the past,"* she said. . . .

Step 2: Team provides Round 1 input

Team members should provide written input. This can be done during a meeting, or with members in different locations. In this first round, each member is providing input without any idea of what other members' inputs or opinions are.

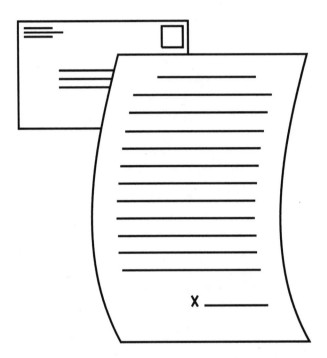

Two weeks before the next board meeting . . .

Betty mailed a letter to each board member. It included a written statement of the decision to be made, and asked each board member to write down *(without consulting others)* his or her definition of the group's purpose/mission. The letter also explained that there would probably be two more rounds coming, during which each member would get to see a summary of what others said, and then provide input again. The members were to mail *(or fax)* their input to Betty so she could summarize it for the upcoming meeting. . . .

Step 3: Summarize Round 1; ask for Round 2 input

You can summarize the results of a round in any of the following ways:

➠ By editing to come up with a synopsis of what the team said as a group *(this can be the most effective method of reaching consensus if the team member inputs are similar).*

➠ By listing the responses verbatim, without editing *(this way the members can gauge exactly what others have said, and how many others are taking certain positions).*

➠ By averaging the responses *(this only applies when your team is providing numerical responses, such as scores, or ratings).*

Betty decided to summarize . . .

the key points and phrases in the team's responses. At the opening of the board meeting, she handed out a copy of the summary to each member. She asked them to each take five minutes to review the summary carefully and to write a new mission statement that reflected both their own views and the collective views of the team. . . .

Here are the team's responses:

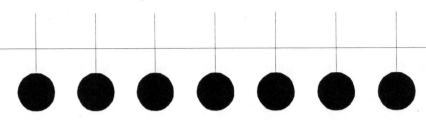

The Charity Service League (CSL) is a nonprofit organization dedicated to:

a. helping those in need:

by giving money

by giving services

by linking them with existing services

b. educating those in need:

by example

through courses

by matching with mentors

c. dispatching/monitoring charity services

d. publicizing what services are available

e. determining who's in need and what they deserve

f. publicizing problems/educating the public

Step 4: Team provides Round 2 input

You may decide to ask for more focused input in the second round, as the team is moving closer to consensus. For example, if you ask members to provide five ideas, or solutions, in the first round, you could then ask them for the *"best"* two or three in the second round.

The board members circled . . .

the ideas they thought were important in Betty's summary and individually rewrote their mission statements. Randy, one of the members asked, *"Do we need to have another round, or can we just have a look now at what we are writing?"* Betty replied, *"Let me take a quick look at what everyone is writing in just a few minutes, and I can summarize it before the end of the meeting. And if our statements are similar, we might not need another round."* A few minutes later, she collected their new mission statements and started to look them over outside the meeting room as the board continued with its agenda. . . .

The Charity Service League (CSL) is a nonprofit organization dedicated to:

a. helping those in need:
~~by giving money~~
(by giving services)
by linking them with existing services

b. educating those in need:
by example
through courses
by matching with mentors

c. dispatching/monitoring charity services

d. ~~publicizing what~~ services are available

e. determining who's in need and what ~~they deserve~~

f. publicizing problems/educating the public

Step 5: Summarize Round 2; ask for Round 3 input

Depending on your team and the issue you are deciding, you may not need to have a third round of inputs from the members.

On the other hand, when dealing with a critical or controversial issue, it might be necessary to continue to a third and maybe even a fourth round. It is in these rounds that members make concessions to work toward a group consensus.

Betty summarized the results . . .

from Round 2 and at the end of the meeting gave out copies of a mission statement that was a composite of those written by the members at the beginning of the meeting. Betty said she felt the mission statement should be more brief and focused, and asked them each to spend five minutes editing this version. . . .

The Charity Service League (CSL) is a non-profit organization dedicated to helping those in need by providing money and services and by connecting individuals to existing charity services. CSL also serves as a clearinghouse of information for both charities and the public. CSL's goal is to educate individuals so they will not need such services in the future.

Step 6: Team provides Round 3 input

If you intend this to be your team's last round, let them know, so they can make sure the input they provide is geared toward arriving at a true team decision.

Each member worked . . .

with the composite statement from the previous round, editing to achieve a consensual statement. They handed their final inputs to Betty, who asked for 10 minutes to summarize this final round. . . .

Step 7: Summarize Round 3

At this point the inputs from the members are close to consensus. Members should have a clear idea of the team's position, although there has been no discussion yet.

If there are still major differences in positions, the team leader (*or whoever is collecting and summarizing inputs*) should recommend another decision-making process to the group (*such as the filtering part of Brainstorming/Filtering, or the Criteria Rating Technique in Chapter Eight*).

Betty noted that the results . . .

were almost identical for Round 3. Therefore, there was no need for another round of voting. Betty formalized this statement and put it on a flip chart for the group to read.

Here is the final version of the Charity Service League's mission statement:

> The Charity Service League is a nonprofit organization dedicated to helping those in need in the short-term, by connecting individuals to existing charity services, and providing long-term assistance toward self-sufficiency.

Step 8: Wrap up the Delphi session

In this step, distribute the final statement to the members. Take appropriate action to:

➠ Communicate the team decision to those who are affected.

➠ Develop a plan to implement the team's decision.

➠ Implement the decision.

➠ Celebrate the fact that a tough decision has been made as a team!

Happy with their new mission statement . . .

the board of the Charity Service League decided to give two awards at the annual banquet. The first was for the individual who helped the most people to become self-sufficient. The second was for the individual who had established links with, and made numerous emergency referrals to, other charity services.

Note: This chapter presented developing a mission statement as an example of using the Delphi Technique. In most cases, however, a team may want to encourage discussion and debate when creating a mission statement. In that case, the Delphi Technique would not be appropriate, as it precludes such discussion, unless you make a point of building it into the last round.

SUMMARY

In summary, use the Delphi Technique to . . .

☑ Ensure anonymity of each member's input in the decision.

☑ Minimize face-to-face interaction, such as when the issue is sensitive or requires confidentiality.

☑ Communicate to each member the collective input of the rest of the team, so they can factor the team's position into their decision.

CHAPTER FIVE WORKSHEET:
USING THE DELPHI TECHNIQUE

1. a) In which specific situations could your team use the Delphi
       Technique?

    _____

    _____

    _____

    b) Why?

    _____

    _____

2. Define the problem to be solved or the decision that needs to be
    made for one of these situations.

    _____

    _____

    _____

3. Who will solicit and summarize the member inputs?

    _____

    _____

4. How many rounds do you think you will need?

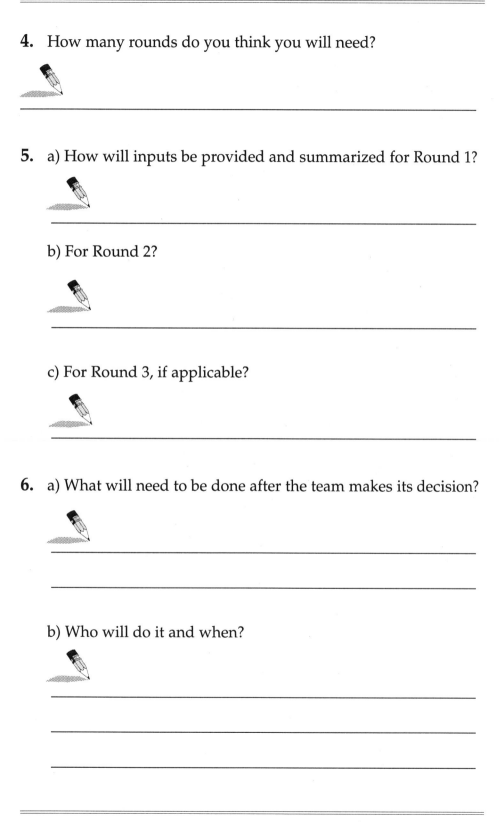

5. a) How will inputs be provided and summarized for Round 1?

_____

b) For Round 2?

_____

c) For Round 3, if applicable?

_____

6. a) What will need to be done after the team makes its decision?

_____

_____

b) Who will do it and when?

_____

_____

_____

CONSENSUS CARD METHOD

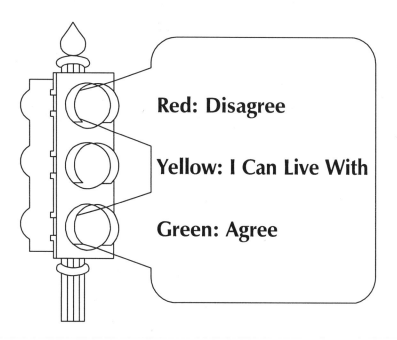

Red: Disagree

Yellow: I Can Live With

Green: Agree

What Is The Consensus Card Method?

Using the Consensus Card Method, everyone in your group employs a visual aid to indicate their position at any point in the discussion. The visual aid, known as the consensus card, is made up of three pieces of colored paper or cardboard folded to form a three-sided shape, like a hollow triangle. Each face of the card is a different color—red, yellow, or green. Each color signifies a different vote as follows:

Red = I disagree and can't commit to support the decision.

Yellow = I can live with the decision and commit to support it.

Green = I agree and commit to support the decision.

Consensus is reached when all team member cards are showing either green or yellow.

When Should The Consensus Card Method Be Used?

You should use the Consensus Card Method to arrive at team decisions when:

☞ **You need opinions voiced and presented in a face-to-face setting.**

☞ **Discussing a complex issue that will elicit complicated and contradictory reactions and opinions from the members of your team.**

☞ **You haven't yet identified what options exist for a particular issue (e.g., *the discussion will be exploring new areas*).**

☞ **You need to bring potential roadblocks into the discussion and get immediate reactions to those roadblocks.**

The Four Steps Of The Consensus Card Method

Step 1: Define the issue and the goal

Step 2: Prepare for the session

Step 3: Present and discuss ideas

Step 4: Wrap up the Consensus Card Method session

Let's look at an example . . .
of the Consensus Card Method in action with the design team at the Human Cycle Bicycle Company. . . .

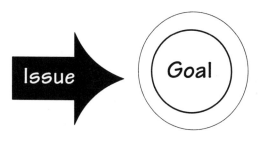

Step 1: Define the issue and the goal

State the issue that needs to be resolved. Set a goal for the session.

The holidays were approaching . . .

and Human Cycle bikes just weren't selling. The president called several key bike stores and found that 90 percent of the customers complained that Human Cycle's bikes were out-of-date. Armed with this information, the president called a meeting of her design team and asked them to decide what the company should do.

Peter, the leader of the design team, was sure any discussion of bike design would spark a heated debate. Therefore, he suggested that the team use the Consensus Card Method to help referee the discussion. The team agreed and set the goal for the upcoming session, namely, to figure out a way to keep Human Cycle Bicycle Company afloat by solving the problem of out-of-date design. . . .

Step 2: Prepare for the session

To prepare for the Consensus Card Method session, you must do three things: set the ground rules and the time frame, explain the use and meaning of the consensus cards, and construct the cards.

Ground rules for the Consensus Card Method

Team members must have a clear view of all others and their consensus cards.

The moderator recognizes speakers and keeps the group from deadlocking.

Allow each individual to fully present his or her idea before recognizing the next speaker.

Ask questions only when you are recognized. (You can be recognized by the team leader or speaker who just presented an idea.)

Feel free to make judgments, but be open-minded and listen to the judgments and opinions of others.

Construct your consensus card

Fold the colored paper or cardboard as indicated and tape it together into a hollow triangle.

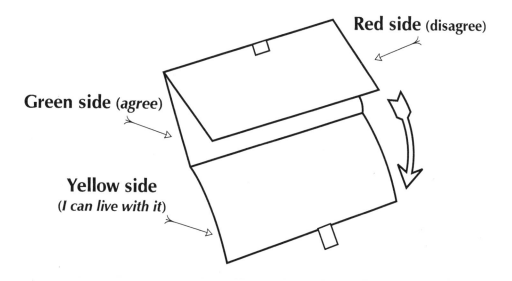

Red side (disagree)

Green side (*agree*)

Yellow side
(*I can live with it*)

Use the card like a personal *"traffic light"* to indicate your position on ideas being discussed. Green means *"yes"* or *"I agree with what is being said."* Red means *"no"* or *"I disagree with what's being said."* Yellow means *"I can live with the decision and commit to support it."*

Before the session begins, each member holds up a card showing the yellow, or neutral position.

When listening, put the green panel up as soon as possible, indicating agreement with the speaker. Don't put up the red panel—meaning stop—until the issue is fully examined and questioned. The goal is to see green and yellow panels facing inward all around the table.

> ## *Peter, the design team leader . . .*
>
> had scheduled a two-hour team meeting. As it began, Peter passed out consensus cards and announced, *"Each of you now holds a personalized traffic light. We have a critical discussion and decision ahead of us this morning. It's important that we get feedback and know where we all stand on the ideas and issues as we move along."*
>
> *"That's where these cards come in. If you have a concern or disagree with the idea on the table, flip your card to show the red side. If you agree, show the green, and if you are neutral, can live with, or want to explore it more, show the yellow side."*
>
> *"Ready to start?"* . . .

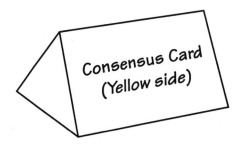

Consensus Card
(Yellow side)

Step 3: Present and discuss ideas

The group presents ideas one at a time on the topic at hand. Discussion of each idea is encouraged. As points are discussed, the team leader acknowledges who agrees with the speaker — that is, who is displaying the green *"agree"* panel on the consensus cards. The leader also notes who disagrees, and who is still neutral or *"can live with"* what's being discussed. The goal is to get as many green panels showing as possible.

As the discussion proceeds, the team leader lists on a flip chart or board all ideas raised.

Warning! If the room fills with green panels quickly, don't assume the solution on the table is the right or only way to reach consensus. There might be a better one yet to come.

If all the team's consensus cards remain on the red face, then the team leader may need to break the deadlock by starting over.

The first speaker, Noah, began with . . .

"*I don't think the design is the problem; the problem is the customers we are trying to attract. If we could find people who fit the Human Cycle image and product, then we should have more success in the marketplace.*" After Noah concluded, two of his teammates were displaying the green face of their consensus cards. Diane, however, started shaking her head and popped the red side of her card up. The other six in the group reserved final judgment and flipped their cards to yellow.

Diane asked, "*What do you mean by new customers? Where do we find them? Who do you think the new customers should be?*"

Noah responded, "*Well, Diane, our current target customers are kids under 18 years old, but I have a feeling the people who would like our designs better are over 35. Look at the overall design, the width of the Human Cycle seat, the range of colors, and the basket on the back.*". . .

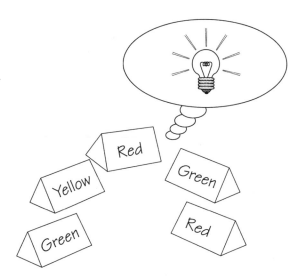

As soon as Noah . . .

clarified the reasoning behind "*the over-35 market,*" the rest of the group flipped their cards to green. Diane flipped hers to yellow, explaining, "*I think our current customer base is already over 35. After all, who pays for a bike for a kid who's 16? Someone over 35!*" When pressed further by other team members, Diane conceded that the Human Cycle bike design could appeal to people over 35. This said, she turned her consensus card to green.

Peter then stopped the group and pointed out, "*Look, we have nearly all greens, a couple of yellows, and no reds. Does that mean we've solved our problem about the design of the Human Cycle bike by changing our target market? If so, this was a pretty easy decision to reach.*". . .

Jeffrey, the top designer, started to laugh . . .

then picked up the discussion by reminding everyone that the real money in the bike business is in children's bikes, not adult bikes. *"Human Cycle should be doing everything it can to attract that market,"* Jeffrey explained, *"If they're 28 and haven't ever bought one of our bikes, they probably never will because they won't be buying another bike for 15 years. However, kids have two or three bikes ahead of them. We should change our design to attract brand loyalty from young customers."*

As Jeffrey stated this opinion, there was a flurry of card changing in the room. Some team members immediately went to red. Most shifted their cards to yellow. The most tolerant remained with the green face up on their cards. Two team members wanted to know how Jeffrey would determine the best new design. Jeffrey gave a quick sketch of a survey and testing process he felt would work well.

Peter reminded the team that they would have a chance to present and discuss more ideas. . . .

Increase Bike Sales

Step 4: Wrap up the Consensus Card Method session

It's time to wrap up when:

> ⇒ All team members display green or yellow on their consensus cards, indicating that consensus has been reached (*providing all ideas have been presented and explored*).
>
> ⇒ The team leader has reviewed all the ideas generated and determined that everyone understands, accepts, and supports the ideas and their implications.
>
> ⇒ You have made a list of the decisions made and agreed on the appropriate next steps.
>
> ⇒ You are certain that no one feels left out or angry.
>
> ⇒ You have thanked the participants for their time and thoughts.

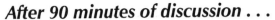
After 90 minutes of discussion . . .

the group realized that they were *"talked out."* Peter read off their list of ideas:

1. Survey kids under 18 and test them on new designs.

2. Target "over-35" buyers for existing bike model advertising. Target "under 18" for new design advertising.

3. Do not manufacture more "over-35" bikes. Alter them as needed over the next year to get them to seem new—so they'll sell out.

4. During the closeout on the original line, come up with two new bikes aimed at the 18 and under crowd.

5. Aim to make the switch-over within five years.

In summary, use the Consensus Card Method to . . .

☑ Handle situations in which diverse and potentially opposing opinions will be voiced in a face-to-face setting.

☑ Arrive at a consensual solution when there are complex and often contradictory issues involved.

☑ Make sure everyone has a chance to express his or her position (*and reasons*) on any alternative presented.

CHAPTER SIX WORKSHEET:
USING THE CONSENSUS CARD METHOD

1. For which specific situations would your team use the
Consensus Card Method?

_____

_____

_____

_____

_____

2. Why?

_____

_____

_____

_____

_____

_____

_____

_____

3. Who will moderate the session? Will this role change from one session to another?

_____

_____

_____

_____

_____

_____

4. For one of the situations identified in question number one *(the decision for which you are most likely to use the Consensus Card Method soon)*, what follow-up action will be necessary?

_____

_____

_____

_____

_____

_____

_____

_____

_____

PAIRED-CHOICE MATRIX

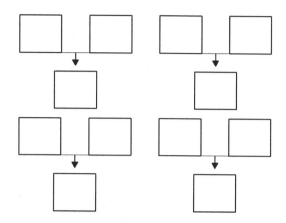

What Is The Paired-Choice Matrix?

The Paired-Choice Matrix allows teams to select from a number of alternatives. Working from a list, you compare pairs of alternatives—until the comparison of pairs produces a single solution. The technique is most often used when there are several *(eight or more)* options on the table.

The best analogy to this is sports league play-offs—in this case, a series of games or matches are played between teams to determine a champion, matching one pair of teams at a time.

When Should The Paired-Choice Matrix Be Used?

The Paired-Choice Matrix can be used when:

☞ **You need to divide a big decision into smaller, easier to manage decisions.**

☞ **You want an objective process to make sure each alternative gets fair and equal consideration as part of the team decision.**

☞ **The alternatives are relatively similar.**

The Six Steps Of The Paired-Choice Matrix

Step 1: Identify the issue, options, and goal

Step 2: Prepare for the session

Step 3: Make decisions between pairs

Step 4: Tally scores of paired choices

Step 5: Discuss and clarify results

Step 6: Wrap up the Paired-Choice Matrix session

Let's see how the Paired-Choice Matrix . . .

was used in the selection of a health care plan at the Spritzing Sprinkler Company. . . .

Issue → Options Options Options → Goal

Step 1: Identify the issue, options, and goal

Determine the issue you need to tackle and the goal you would like to reach. Collect a list of options that you must decide from in order to reach your goal.

The employees of the Spritzing Sprinkler Company . . .

were at an impasse with their health care provider. The provider wanted to increase their rates by 35 percent, and their policy was set to expire on January 1. Since a 35 percent increase was clearly unacceptable to management and Spritzing's 250 employees, the company decided to form a team to research and select a new health plan.

The president asked for volunteers from five departments. Barbara, Millie, Manuel, Steve, and Charlie responded to the call.

At their first meeting, the team elected Barbara as their leader. Barbara then assigned each member the task of researching two health care plans. . . .

Step 2: Prepare for the session

Prepare for the session by laying out a chart that will serve as the matrix for comparing pairs of options. The chart should look like this:

	Alternative A	Alternative B	Alternative C	Alternative D	Alternative N
Alternative A	███				
Alternative B	X	███			
Alternative C	X	X	███		
Alternative D	X	X	X	███	
Alternative N	X	X	X	X	███

Explain the process to your group. List the options along the top and down the side of the chart in the same order, starting with the first row. Move horizontally across the chart, comparing the first option to every option along the top line, one pair at a time. Indicate the team's choice for each pair in the corresponding box. The process is repeated until each possible pair is compared (*all the boxes above the diagonal line are marked*). The option that gets the greatest number of *"preferred"* votes wins.

> ### *At the second meeting of the team . . .*
>
> Barbara asked for the list of health care plans that were available and wrote each one in a box along the top and sides of the Paired-Choice Matrix she had drawn on a flip chart before the meeting began. Barbara explained that the team would be comparing each plan to the others, and in that way they would be making several choices between all the possible pairs of choices.
>
> Next Barbara asked each team member to give a report on the health care plans they had investigated. . . .

Step 3: Make decisions between pairs

The leader reviews each pair of options and asks for a show of hands regarding the preference. The leader records whatever choice prevails—not the number of votes. The leader repeats the voting for each pair of options above the diagonal line on the chart.

Barbara asked for a show of hands . . .

as she compared the first set of pairs, *"Plan A and Plan B."* The group favored Plan B four to one so Barbara recorded a B in the box where the two items *"intersected."*

She then proceeded across the row for Plan A and asked for a show of hands regarding Plan A versus Plan C. The group favored C by a margin of three to two. Again Barbara simply recorded C in the corresponding box.

Barbara continued the voting for each row until she came up with the following results:

	A	B	C	D	E	F	G	Total
A	■	B	C	D	A	F	G	1
B	X	■	B	D	B	B	B	4
C	X	X	■	C	C	F	G	2
D	X	X	X	■	D	F	D	2
E	X	X	X	X	■	F	G	0
F	X	X	X	X	X	■	G	0
G	X	X	X	X	X	X	■	0
Total	-	1	1	2	0	4	4	■

Step 4: Tally scores of paired choices

For each horizontal line, tally the number of times that choice prevailed. Record those numbers on the right side of the chart. Tally the scores for each column as well, recording the scores on the bottom of the matrix. Again, whichever option has the greatest number of *"preferences"* is the top choice. If there is a tie, then you could:

➠ Ask for a vote by the team on the best choice *(if it is a tie between two options)*.

➠ Repeat the process with a smaller chart that includes this short list of options *(if there are three or more options with the same score)*.

Similarly, if there are two or more choices that are very close, you can use the Criteria Rating Technique, which is described in the next chapter.

Barbara tallied the scores . . .
horizontally and vertically, added them together for each option, and came up with the following:

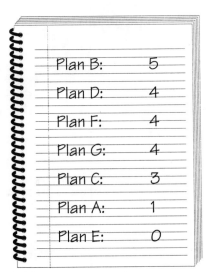

Plan B: 5
Plan D: 4
Plan F: 4
Plan G: 4
Plan C: 3
Plan A: 1
Plan E: 0

The group could see . . .

that Plan B was the top choice. However, since the voting was so close—five for Plan B and a three-way tie for second place, Barbara felt she should make sure the team had reached a decision they could all support and live with. She had the team repeat the Paired-Choice Matrix quickly for the top four and there was clear consensus on Plan B. . . .

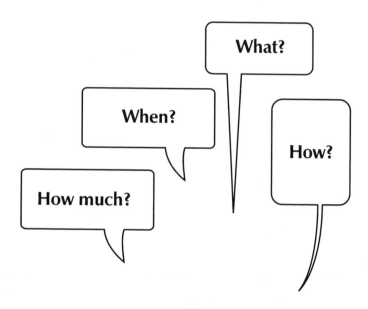

Step 5: Discuss and clarify results

Review the final choice and discuss what that selection means to your group. Ask the following questions: what, when, how, and how much?

Barbara asked Steve . . .

to state for the group which plan had been chosen and why. Steve said, *"We chose Plan B by comparing the relative benefits of the seven plans. Clearly our group felt that Plan B's deductible was preferable, despite the slightly longer waiting period."* The group concurred. Barbara exclaimed, *"I can't believe we made such a difficult decision in 35 minutes. Without this technique it would have taken hours."*. . .

Step 6: Wrap up the Paired-Choice Matrix session

It's time to wrap up when:

→ There are no more decisions to be made.

→ The group understands what has been chosen and why.

→ Team members have been thanked for their ideas and time.

Barbara wrote a memo . . .
to the company president that she could copy and forward to everyone, describing their final selection and the method they used to find it. Once she sent it off, she felt confident that they would all have new health coverage before their current plan expired.

In summary, use the Paired-Choice Matrix when . . .

☑ You have a large or complex group of alternatives to evaluate in a short amount of time.

☑ The options being compared are similar.

☑ You need to break a complicated problem down into simple steps.

The Paired-Choice Matrix can be used in combination with other tools in this guidebook. For example, you can use brainstorming to develop the list of choices for the matrix. Or, if the Paired-Choice Matrix produces a set of solutions *(more than two)* that are all equal, then you might want to try the Criteria Rating Technique *(in the next chapter)*, as a way to make your final, informed, and unbiased choice.

CHAPTER SEVEN WORKSHEET
USING THE PAIRED-CHOICE MATRIX

1. For which specific situations would your team use the Paired-Choice Matrix?

_____

_____

_____

_____

_____

_____

_____

_____

2. How many alternatives would be compared in these situations?

_____

_____

_____

_____

_____

_____

3. a) How will the team make a final decision in the event of a tie
or very close scores?

_____

_____

_____

_____

_____

_____

_____

b) Why?

_____

_____

_____

_____

_____

_____

_____

_____

_____

CRITERIA RATING TECHNIQUE

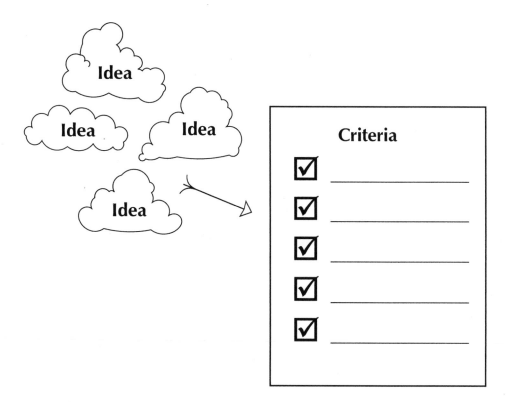

What Is The Criteria Rating Technique?

The Criteria Rating Technique is a decision-making tool teams use to arrive at a choice between alternatives, using clearly defined criteria to make their decisions.

When Should The Criteria Rating Technique Be Used?

Use the Criteria Rating Technique when:

☞ **The team has to select from several alternatives and it is important to focus on why choices are being made the way they are.**

☞ **You want to make sure the team makes the decision objectively** *(appropriate when there are strong opinions involved).*

☞ **You want the team to arrive at a decision that members can support and be able to communicate to others the rationale behind the decision.**

☞ **You need to make a decision based on a short list from a Brainstorming/Filtering or Paired-Choice Matrix session.**

Criteria

☑ _____

☑ _____

☑ _____

☑ _____

☑ _____

The Seven Steps Of The Criteria Rating Technique

Step 1: Start the session and list the alternatives

Step 2: Brainstorm decision criteria

Step 3: Determine the relative importance of each criterion

Step 4: Establish a rating scale, then rate the alternatives

Step 5: Calculate the final score

Step 6: Select the best alternative

Step 7: Wrap up the Criteria Rating Technique session

Now let's look at a real-life example . . .

of use of the Criteria Rating Technique at Radio Station KEAR-FM. A team was having trouble making a decision about which new employee to hire for a consolidated job in the *"audience development area."*

The station couldn't afford to hire and train the wrong person, nor could they afford a long, highly political interviewing process. This would be hard to avoid since Charlene, the station head, was bombarded with requests to consider friends and relatives of assorted station employees.

To keep things fair and simple, Charlene decided to use the Criteria Rating Technique to select the best person for the job. She knew it could help her and the hiring team objectively evaluate the short list of candidates for the job. . . .

Step 1: Start the session and list the alternatives

At the start of your Criteria Rating Technique session:

> ⇒ Provide a time limit for the session. Generally 45 to 60 minutes is sufficient.
>
> ⇒ Prepare a blank Criteria Rating Form on a flip chart or an overhead transparency.
>
> ⇒ List alternatives or options available along the top of the Criteria Rating Form.
>
> **Note:** You may have to generate these options or alternatives by brainstorming.

On Tuesday afternoon . . .

Charlene and her interview team completed their interviews and came up with a short list of three top candidates—Billy, Inez, and Vance. On Wednesday morning, she called a meeting of her hiring team, distributed the three top candidates' resumes, and announced that the group would make a decision on the candidates in the next 50 minutes. Charlene explained that they would use the Criteria Rating Technique because it would allow them to evaluate the candidates objectively.

Bruce, a team member, wondered how the Criteria Rating Technique could ensure objectivity. Charlene asked him to look closely at the Criteria Rating Form she taped to the wall. She asked him to note the two column headings on the left: one for criteria and one for weight. The criteria for this job at KEAR would be the skill and experience requirements found in the job description. The weight would be the relative importance the group attached to each quality or skill. . . .

Step 2: Brainstorm decision criteria

You will be judging your alternatives against the most important qualities each alternative should have. These qualities are called decision criteria. Everyone uses decision criteria in all aspects of life.

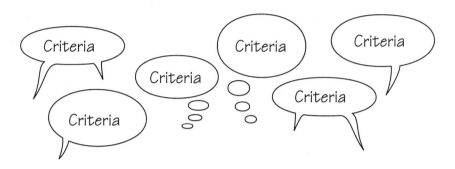

For example, when you and your significant other want to rent an apartment, you consider a whole range of issues (*or decision criteria*) such as price, location, size, number of bathrooms, neighbors above and below, security, school system, rent control, condition of space, length of the lease, and the amount of money you have to put down, not to mention whether your landlord will ever lift a finger to call a plumber.

If you see an apartment alone, you might think neighbors, price, and security are the most important things to consider when choosing an apartment. In contrast, if your significant other visits a different apartment alone, he or she might value rent control, bathrooms, and landlord availability, and select what you consider the wrong apartment for the two of you. To prevent a fight, you might find it helpful to jointly develop a list of criteria you consider most important and use these decision criteria to evaluate different apartments.

Here are some common categories for selection criteria in the context of your work:

Selection Criteria

➡ Ease of implementation

➡ Lowest cost

➡ Ability to meet customer requirements

➡ Resource availability

➡ Lowest risk

➡ Fastest to implement

➡ Long-term workability

Remember, the criteria may change for each project or problem you are working on. This list notes general areas of concern.

Your group can determine decision criteria through Brainstorming/ Filtering *(see Chapter Three for guidelines)*.

Charlene pulled out . . .

the job description for the position and read it to the group. She then asked them to break down the description into qualities and skills that could be listed on separate lines of the criteria section of the Criteria Rating Form.

Here is the list of necessary qualities for the new employee regarding the audience development job:

Necessary Qualities

✔ Self-starter

✔ Good public relations/marketing skills

✔ Articulate

✔ Good writing skills

✔ Creative problem solver

✔ Outreach experience

✔ Managed public relations/marketing on a day-to-day basis

✔ Handle and create budgets

✔ Good organizational skills

✔ Able to analyze existing markets and target new ones

✔ Good research skills

✔ Delegation skills

✔ Ability to prioritize

✔ Team player

Step 3: Determine the relative importance of each criterion

➠ Give each criterion a weight *(that represents its relative importance).*

➠ To determine the weight of each criterion, ask, *"How important is each criterion in relation to the others?"*

➠ Remember that the total of the assigned weights for all criteria must equal 100 percent.

Criteria	Weight (%)
Self-starter	15
Good public relations/marketing skills	20
Good writing skills	10
Creative problem solver	15
Delegation skills	15
Able to analyze existing markets and target new ones	25

Charlene asked the team . . .

to review the criteria and decide how important each quality or skill was in relation to the others. She asked them to assign each criterion a percentage that represented its priority *(e.g., 3 percent would mean a low priority and 90 percent a high priority).* She reminded everyone that the total of their priorities had to equal 100 percent. Charlene gave them seven minutes to rate the list. The group also decided to combine some criteria and to eliminate a few entirely. . . .

Step 4: Establish a rating scale, then rate the alternatives

First establish the rating scale you will use. A consistent rating scale must be used to compare the various ideas or alternatives against each criterion. Any scale will work as long as the same scale is used for all alternatives and criteria. A ten-point rating scale, with ten being highest, is common.

Each idea or alternative should be rated against each criterion using the established rating scale. It should not be rated against the other items being evaluated. It is possible that the rating can only be determined after an investigation.

After the team agreed . . .

on the weights for the criteria, they began the process of rating each candidate for the job against the criteria. They decided to use a ten-point rating scale with 10 being highest . . . .

Step 5: Calculate the final score

To calculate the final score and determine the team's decision:

➠ Multiply the weight *(established in Step 3)* by the rating for each alternative *(established in Step 4)*.

➠ Write this figure in parenthesis in the appropriate box on the Criteria Rating Form.

➠ Add the numbers in parenthesis for each alternative and write the total in the appropriate box.

➠ Write any summary comments in the appropriate box.

Criteria Rating Form						
		Rating Scale: 1 *(low)* **to 10** *(high)*				
		Alternatives *(Candidates)*				
		A Billy	**B** Inez	**C** Vance	**D** —	**E** —
Criteria	**Weight**					
Self-starter	15%	3 (.45)	5 (.75)	6 (.90)		
PR/Marketing Skills	20%	8 (1.6)	8 (1.6)	7 (1.4)		
Writing Skills	10%	6 (.60)	7 (.70)	6 (.60)		
Creative Problem Solver	15%	8 (1.2)	8 (1.2)	7 (1.05)		
Delegation Skills	15%	4 (.60)	6 (.90)	6 (.90)		
Market Analysis and Targeting	25%	8 (2.0)	9 (2.25)	9 (2.25)		
Total Points	**100%**	37 (6.45)	43 (7.40)	41 (7.10)		

I
Charlene asked Debbie . . .
to multiply the weight for each criterion by the rating given to each candidate in the group. The team then added the weighted and unweighted scores for each candidate. . . .

Step 6: Select the best alternative

Select the alternative that has the highest total score. However, be aware that this alternative may or may not be the one ultimately chosen. The alternative with the highest score should be the best. If the team members don't agree, they should review the weighting of the criteria and the ratings, and make necessary changes.

I
On the basis of the weighting . . .
the group established and the rating they gave to each candidate, Inez seemed to be the best candidate for the audience development job at KEAR-FM. Charlene asked, *"Is everyone comfortable with the decision?"* Bruce responded, *"I'm not sure she would have been my choice if we had just sat around the table and talked about our favorites, but based on the way we made the decision, I agree 100 percent."*. . .

Step 7: Wrap up the Criteria Rating Technique session

You know it's time to stop the Criteria Rating Technique session when:

➠ Your group has come to an agreement on the *"best"* alternative.

➠ Assignments have been made to communicate the group's final decision.

➠ Assignments have been made *(if necessary)* to implement the team's decision.

➠ You have thanked the participants.

Now that the group . . .

had their top candidate, they decided to check her references. Debbie volunteered to check references and Bruce offered to help. If there were no problems or inconsistencies, the group authorized Charlene to make the offer to Inez.

In summary, use the Criteria Rating Technique to . . .

☑ Select from among several alternatives. *(The Criteria Rating Technique will help the decision-making process by providing a step-by-step procedure.)*

☑ Build more objectivity into the decision-making process. *(The Criteria Rating Technique takes subjectivity out of the decision-making process by assigning weights and rankings to each potential solution.)*

☑ Build consensus while depersonalizing individual contributions. *(The Criteria Rating Technique helps to build consensus by taking "opinion" out of the decision-making process.)*

CHAPTER EIGHT WORKSHEET:
USING THE CRITERIA RATING TECHNIQUE

1. For which specific decisions would your team use the Criteria Rating Technique?

_____

_____

_____

_____

_____

2. a) How many criteria would you use?

_____

_____

b) What would those criteria be?

_____

_____

_____

_____

_____

3. What would the weightings be?

_____

_____

_____

_____

_____

_____

_____

4. How would your team decide in the event of a tie?

_____

_____

_____

_____

_____

_____

_____

_____

_____

CHAPTER NINE

SUMMARY

In this guidebook we learned various techniques and tools for teams to be more successful at making decisions.

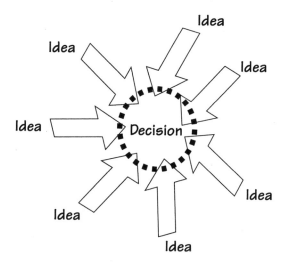

Brainstorming/Filtering stimulates creativity. After generating choices by brainstorming, use a set of filters to select the best options. Brainstorming can be used alone or in combination with other techniques.

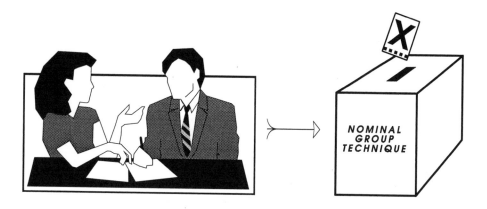

The **Nominal Group Technique** combines aspects of silent voting with limited, face-to-face discussion. This technique is often used when you want to ensure everyone has an equal opportunity to participate in the decision.

Round 1	Round 2	Round 3
Input	Input	Input
Input	Input	
Input	Input	
Input	Input	
Input		
Input		
Input		

The **Delphi Technique** involves anonymous solicitation and comparison of multiple rounds of inputs, and feedback of summaries of those inputs. Use this method when team members are far apart physically and you need to remove the bias that may occur in personal contact.

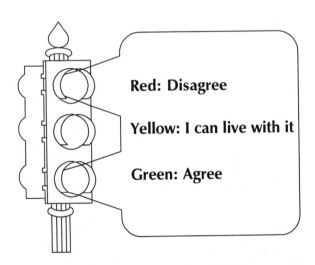

Red: Disagree

Yellow: I can live with it

Green: Agree

Use the **Consensus Card Method** when you want to continuously monitor each person's position on an issue. The consensus card is a visual aid each individual uses as a personal *"traffic light."*

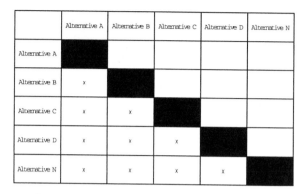

	Alternative A	Alternative B	Alternative C	Alternative D	Alternative N
Alternative A	■				
Alternative B	x	■			
Alternative C	x	x	■		
Alternative D	x	x	x	■	
Alternative N	x	x	x	x	■

The **Paired-Choice Matrix** is an organized way of deciding among similar alternatives. Your group makes a series of choices between pairs until you eliminate all inappropriate options.

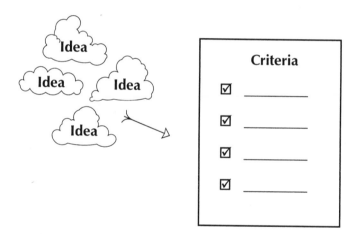

The **Criteria Rating Technique** allows you to objectively evaluate alternatives against your group's criteria. It's a valuable tool to deal with complex or lingering team decisions/problems.

All of these tools are effective and you, as a team member, need to know how to use them and when to apply them. These decision-making techniques will make your team function more effectively. They can help you discover problems, analyze alternatives, find solutions to problems, and make lasting decisions. By using these techniques, you will increase group harmony and efficiency. And you will make better team decisions.

REPRODUCIBLE FORMS

The following forms are provided for you to photocopy and use appropriately.

Paired-Choice Matrix

	■						
	X	■					
	X	X	■				
	X	X	X	■			
	X	X	X	X	■		
	X	X	X	X	X	■	
	X	X	X	X	X	X	■

Criteria Rating Form						
		Rating Scale: 1 (low) **to 10** (high)				
		Alternatives				
Criteria	**Weight**	**A**	**B**	**C**	**D**	**E**
Total Points	**100%**					

Professional And Personal Development Publications From Richard Chang Associates, Inc.

Designed to support continuous learning, these highly targeted, integrated collections from Richard Chang Associates, Inc. (RCA) help individuals and organizations acquire the knowledge and skills needed to succeed in today's ever-changing workplace. Titles are available through RCA, Jossey-Bass, Inc., fine bookstores, and distributors internationally.

Practical Guidebook Collection

Quality Improvement Series
Continuous Process Improvement
Continuous Improvement Tools, Volume 1
Continuous Improvement Tools, Volume 2
Step-By-Step Problem Solving
Meetings That Work!
Improving Through Benchmarking
Succeeding As A Self-Managed Team
Measuring Organizational Improvement Impact
Process Reengineering In Action
Satisfying Internal Customers First!

Management Skills Series
Interviewing And Selecting High Performers
On-The-Job Orientation And Training
Coaching Through Effective Feedback
Expanding Leadership Impact
Mastering Change Management
Re-Creating Teams During Transitions
Planning Successful Employee Performance
Coaching For Peak Employee Performance
Evaluating Employee Performance

High Performance Team Series
Success Through Teamwork
Building A Dynamic Team
Measuring Team Performance
Team Decision-Making Techniques

High-Impact Training Series
Creating High-Impact Training
Identifying Targeted Training Needs
Mapping A Winning Training Approach
Producing High-Impact Learning Tools
Applying Successful Training Techniques
Measuring The Impact Of Training
Make Your Training Results Last

Workplace Diversity Series
Capitalizing On Workplace Diversity
Successful Staffing In A Diverse Workplace
Team Building For Diverse Work Groups
Communicating In A Diverse Workplace
Tools For Valuing Diversity

Personal Growth And Development Collection

Managing Your Career in a Changing Workplace
Unlocking Your Career Potential
Marketing Yourself and Your Career
Making Career Transitions
Memory Tips For The Forgetful

101 Stupid Things Collection

101 Stupid Things Trainers Do To Sabotage Success
101 Stupid Things Supervisors Do To Sabotage Success
101 Stupid Things Employees Do To Sabotage Success
101 Stupid Things Salespeople Do To Sabotage Success
101 Stupid Things Business Travelers Do To Sabotage Success

About Richard Chang Associates, Inc.

Richard Chang Associates, Inc. (RCA) is a multi-disciplinary organizational performance improvement firm. Since 1987, RCA has provided private and public sector clients around the world with the experience, expertise, and resources needed to build capability in such critical areas as process improvement, management development, project management, team performance, performance measurement, and facilitator training. RCA's comprehensive package of services, products, and publications reflect the firm's commitment to practical, innovative approaches and to the achievement of significant, measurable results.

RCA Resources Optimize Organizational Performance

Consulting — Using a broad range of skills, knowledge, and tools, RCA consultants assist clients in developing and implementing a wide range of performance improvement initiatives.

Training — Practical, "real world" training programs are designed with a "take initiative" emphasis. Options include off-the-shelf programs, customized programs, and public and on-site seminars.

Curriculum And Materials Development — A cost-effective and flexible alternative to internal staffing, RCA can custom-develop and/or customize content to meet both organizational objectives and specific program needs.

Video Production — RCA's award-winning, custom video productions provide employees with information in a consistent manner that achieves lasting impact.

Publications — The comprehensive and practical collection of publications from RCA support organizational training initiatives and self-directed learning.

Packaged Programs — Designed for first-time and experienced trainers alike, these program offer comprehensive, integrated materials (including selected Practical Guidebooks) that provide wide range of flexible training options. Choose from:

- Meetings That Work! ToolPAK™
- Step-By-Step Problem Solving ToolKIT™
- Continuous Process Improvement Packaged Training Program
- Continuous Improvement Tools, Volume 1 ToolPAK™
- Continuous Improvement Tools, Volume 2 ToolPAK™
- High Involvement Teamwork™ Packaged Training Program

RICHARD
CHANG
ASSOCIATES

World Class Resources. World Class Results.^{SM}

Richard Chang Associates, Inc.
Corporate Headquarters
15265 Alton Parkway, Suite 300, Irvine, California 92618 USA
(800) 756-8096 • (949) 727-7477 • Fax: (949) 727-7007
E-Mail: info@rca4results.com • www.richardchangassociates.com

U.S. Offices in Irvine and Atlanta • Licensees and Distributors Worldwide